What Is the Story of Dracula?

by Michael Burgan

illustrated by David Malan

Penguin Workshop

PENGUIN WORKSHOP
An Imprint of Penguin Random House LLC, New York

© Universal City Studios LLC. All Rights Reserved.
Published in 2020 by Penguin Workshop, an imprint of Penguin Random House LLC, New York.
PENGUIN and PENGUIN WORKSHOP are trademarks of Penguin Books Ltd.
WHO HQ & Design is a registered trademark of Penguin Random House LLC.
Printed in the USA.

Visit us online at www.penguinrandomhouse.com.

Library of Congress Control Number: 2019054706

ISBN 9781524788452 (paperback)   10 9 8 7 6 5 4 3 2 1
ISBN 9781524788469 (library binding)   10 9 8 7 6 5 4 3 2 1

Contents

What Is the Story of Dracula?

Moviegoers crowded New York City's Roxy Theatre on February 12, 1931. The entertainment that day included a musical play and film clips of recent news. But the audience in the Roxy was eager to see the feature film—a story many of them already knew. It was the tale of Count Dracula, who left his homeland of Transylvania and sailed to England. Why did he take this journey? He wanted blood—human blood!

The actor Bela Lugosi played the count in the film. Though he was hundreds of years old, Dracula never seemed to age. And on-screen, Lugosi's hair was dark and slicked back. He wore a tuxedo and a cape, and as a guest entered his castle, he said with an accent, "I am Dracula. I bid you welcome." Wolves howled in the distance as Dracula's ghoulish story began.

In the 1931 film *Dracula*, audiences heard the vampire speak on-screen for the first time. They saw him turn into a bat in his search of victims.

And they watched the vampire slayer Professor Van Helsing drive a wooden stake into him.

By the time the film version of *Dracula* was released, the story of this ageless vampire was already known around the world. Vampire tales had been told for centuries, scaring children and adults alike. Imagine humans who are dead but don't stay that way. Instead, some mysterious, evil force lets them live forever, as long as they drink blood. And as long as they can avoid the living people who want to kill them once and for all.

Those tales of vampires influenced an Irish writer named Bram Stoker. He created what would become the most famous idea of a vampire ever—Dracula. Stoker's book about the Transylvanian count was published in 1897 and was soon translated into other languages.

Van Helsing's stake killed Dracula. But only in the movie. For fans of his story, Dracula will never die. People like scary books and films too much. And they seem to love vampires! Since the 1931 movie, Stoker's story has been retold many times and inspired new vampire tales. But Dracula is the vampire most people know best. Today, he's still one of fiction's most fascinating, and terrifying, characters.

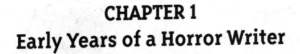

CHAPTER 1
Early Years of a Horror Writer

While other children in Artane, Ireland, ran and played outside, Abraham Stoker could only watch. Until the age of seven, the boy could not walk. He never left his bed. Doctors found no medical reason for his mysterious condition.

Bram, as he was later known, was born on November 8, 1847, in Clontarf, not far from Ireland's capital of Dublin. He lived in nearby Artane with his parents, Abraham Stoker Sr. and Charlotte, and his four brothers and two sisters. Mr. Stoker worked for the Irish government, while Bram's mother raised the children. She was a strong influence on young Bram.

Though Bram could not walk during his early years, he read the books his mother brought him. And he listened to her tell Irish folktales filled with fairies and other magical characters. But not all her stories were make-believe. And some of them were truly horrible.

The Wail of the Banshee and the Death Coach

One of the most famous characters in Irish folktales is the banshee. She is a female spirit who is said to let out a loud cry just before someone dies. Some people say that her cry also calls out a spirit known as the Dullahan. He is the headless driver of a coach, or wagon, pulled by black horses. In the back of his coach is a coffin. When the Dullahan and his Death Coach stop in front of a house, it means someone inside is about to die, and he will take that person away.

Some stories say that if people open the door of their house to the coach driver, he will throw a bucket of blood in their face! Today, people in Ireland know the banshee and the Dullahan are not real. But when Bram Stoker's mother was a child, many people did believe the tales.

Mrs. Stoker said that she had heard the wail of the banshee before her own mother's death.

When Mrs. Stoker was a teenager in Sligo, Ireland, a deadly disease called cholera spread throughout the region. More than half the people in the area died from this severe stomach infection. Mrs. Stoker told her children what she had seen and heard during those dark times. When a traveler to town suddenly showed signs of the disease, the people pushed him into a pit while he was still alive and covered him with dirt! Sometimes, people were even placed in their coffins or thrown onto piles of dead bodies while they were still alive.

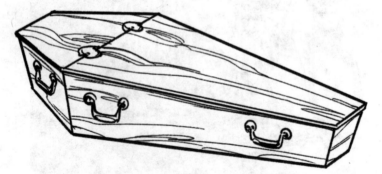

Bram never said what he thought of these stories. But as an adult, he asked his mother to write them down. The idea that people might be buried before they were dead fueled the imagination of the man who went on to write *Dracula.*

When Bram was seven years old, the strange condition that had kept him from walking suddenly improved. He began to go to school and play sports. He also went to see plays with his father, and he developed a great love of the theater. Bram especially liked holiday

plays called pantos. Many of these plays were based on fairy tales or stories from popular books.

After graduating in 1870 from Trinity College in Dublin, Bram Stoker worked for a time in the government, like his father. He also began his writing career. His first published articles were reviews of local plays. Then, in 1872, he published a short story titled "The Crystal Cup." The strange story is about an artist who is locked up in a castle and forced to work for a greedy king.

Bram continued to write about magical people and events. In 1881, he wrote a book of fairy tales called *Under the Sunset*. The characters included angels and evil spirits. By then, Bram had a new full-time job in London. He managed the business

of a well-known actor named Henry Irving. And in his spare time, he still wrote books.

Henry Irving

CHAPTER 2
Vampires Everywhere!

Bram Stoker probably had heard of earlier vampire tales when he was a young boy. The idea that some people die but can still walk the earth has been part of myths and folktales for centuries. These people are often called the undead.

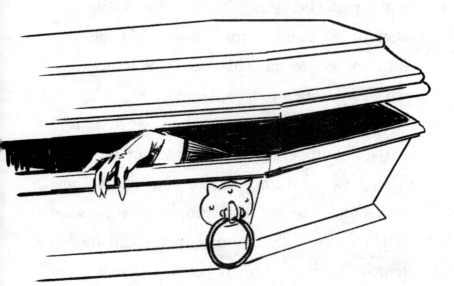

The undead include creatures such as zombies, ghosts, mummies, and vampires. An evil spirt of some kind keeps them from dying completely and drives them to harm the living. What sets vampires apart from other undead is their need for blood from a living person.

Blood-sucking undead creatures of early folktales included the *jiangshi* of China. They walked with stiff arms and usually had greenish skin. In parts of what are now the African nations of Ghana and Togo, some people told tales of the Adze, a spirit that could take the form of an insect and then bite its victims, which were often young children.

Starting about five hundred years ago in parts of Europe, people talked about vampires. They believed there were many ways to become one. Some thought that people who drowned might never really die, that they could instead remain "undead." Others believed that if a cat, dog, or living person walked over a new grave, the person buried there might become a vampire.

Jiangshi

In some European legends, vampires were said to be thin, with scabs covering their bodies. Their skin was deathly pale—until they drank the blood they needed so badly. Since vampires were not truly dead, their hair and nails continued to grow. The tales also said that vampires were incredibly strong and could change into the shape of other animals, such as wolves.

A vampire was strongest at night, and some stories said sunlight would actually kill one. In some countries, though, people believed vampires could go out during the day, but they lost their superhuman powers in daylight.

People also talked about how to keep vampires away. The strong smell of garlic was thought to work, and people were told to spread it around windows and doors. A cross, or even just the sign of a cross, was also said to turn away vampires. Vampire tales also discussed how to make these undead creatures really dead, once and for all. The methods included cutting off the vampire's head or driving a sharp wooden stake through its heart. A shot through the heart with a silver bullet blessed by a priest could also do the job.

Starting in the 1800s, some writers in England began including vampires in their poetry. But

the first full-length story about one in English is thought to be *The Vampyre*, by John Polidori. It was published in a magazine in 1819. The vampire's name is Lord Ruthven, and Polidori wrote he had "dead grey" eyes and pale skin.

John Polidori

Several decades passed before another popular vampire story was written in English. *Varney the Vampire, or, The Feast of Blood* by James Malcolm Rymer was published in London in 1847. The novel had first appeared as more than two hundred chapters that were published separately as booklets.

These short tales were known as penny dreadfuls because they cost just a penny and often told tales of bloody horror.

In this story, Varney travels from central Europe to England and begins seeking out young victims. He climbs into their rooms at night while they sleep. Varney has fangs that leave two bite marks on his victims' necks. And he can climb down stone walls.

Many animals have been associated with vampires, but the most famous is the bat.

A Night of Ghost Stories

John Polidori's tale of Ruthven the vampire sprang from a challenge given by Lord George Gordon Byron, an English poet. In June 1816, Lord Byron and some friends were staying at a house near Lake Geneva in Switzerland. One night, Byron suggested they each try to write a ghost story. Polidori took a rough idea Byron had written

and turned it into *The Vampyre*. The challenge that night to write a scary story led to another important book. One of Byron's other guests was a young Englishwoman named Mary Wollstonecraft Shelley. The story she began writing in Switzerland was the beginning of her famous novel: *Frankenstein*, which she published in 1818.

Plenty for a Penny

By the 1830s, more and more people were learning to read. British publishers began printing short stories that quickly became wildly popular. They were priced to appeal to working-class people who could not afford more expensive books.

For a penny, readers could buy dramatic stories about thieves, detectives, pirates, and sometimes supernatural creatures, like the one in *Varney the Vampire*. These slim booklets, printed on inexpensive paper, were often called penny bloods or penny awfuls. Today they're better known as penny dreadfuls. Each booklet was eight or sixteen pages long and had an illustration on the first page to catch readers' attention.

One booklet contained only a part of the story.

If readers wanted to know what happened, they had to buy the next edition in the series. The longest series of penny dreadfuls was called *Mysteries of London*. It was published over twelve years and contained more than four million words!

A few hundred years before Bram Stoker was even born, Spanish explorers had seen bats in Mexico and South and Central America that they believed drank the blood of other animals. The Spaniards knew the tales about human vampires, and they called the bats they saw vampire bats. Bram had read about vampire bats. He may have also heard older tales that linked vampires and bats, and became the first writer to tell a story about a vampire who turns into one.

As for vampire bats—they don't actually suck their victims' blood. Instead, they cut an animal's skin with their teeth, then lick up the blood as it oozes out. But they can't go too long without it, just like the vampire characters in folktales.

CHAPTER 3
Writing *Dracula*

In March 1890, Bram Stoker began scribbling the first notes for his vampire story. That summer, he traveled to Whitby, England. The town sits

on the North Sea. He wasn't there to enjoy the beach, though. Bram continued the research for his vampire book. Some of the well-known parts of *Dracula* came from his time in Whitby. The town itself is featured in the book. The sites he mentions include the ruins of an old church and

its nearby cemetery. He studied the gravestones there, and Swales, the name of one of Dracula's first victims, came from one of them.

When he first started writing, Bram called his vampire Count Wampyr. *Wampyr* is the German word for *vampire*. But then he found the now-famous name in a book in the Whitby library. He learned that a region of Romania called Wallachia had once been the home of a fifteenth-century ruler named Vlad Tepes—

who was also known as Dracula. In the local language, the name meant "son of Dracul," and *dracul* can mean either a devil or dragon. Soon, Stoker was making changes to his notes. He crossed out every mention of *Count Wampyr* and wrote in *Dracula*.

Vlad Tepes

Who was the real Dracula? He was a prince who defended his people from attack by Turkish armies. He was also known as Vlad the Impaler, because he often speared his enemies on large wooden stakes. Stoker did not seem to know all this history, but one character in the book mentions that Count Dracula was most likely the ruler who battled the Turks.

What Bram Stoker read in Whitby, and while doing later research about Vlad Tepes, convinced him to change his vampire's home country to Transylvania. That region of Romania is near Wallachia. Transylvania was once part of Hungary, where tales of vampires were common. And an actual blood drinker once lived there—a

Hungarian countess named Elizabeth Báthory. The countess believed the blood of young women kept her youthful.

Over the next several years, Bram Stoker continued working for Henry Irving. When he had time, Bram researched and wrote his vampire book. When he finished it, he turned it over to his publisher with the title *The Un-Dead*. In May 1897, the book appeared in London bookstores. Before then, either Bram or his publisher had decided to change the title. The book about the count from Transylvania was now titled *Dracula*.

Learning about Vampires

One of Bram Stoker's most important sources was *The Land Beyond the Forest*. It was written in 1888 by a Scottish writer named Emily Gerard.

The title refers to the English meaning of the word *Transylvania*—"across the forest." Gerard had lived in Transylvania for several years. In her book, she described in detail some of the folktales and legends of Transylvania. One of

them said that the devil ran a school in the mountains where he taught humans magical spells! Another was the Transylvanians' strong belief in vampires and the idea that someone bitten by a vampire becomes one, too. Gerard also mentioned that one Romanian word for a vampire is *nosferatu*.

CHAPTER 4
Hunting a Vampire

Dracula starts with a journal entry by Jonathan Harker. He is one of the English lawyers Count Dracula has hired to help buy him a house just outside London. The journal entry reveals how Bram wrote the book: from the point of view of the different main characters. Readers learn details of the story from the characters' diaries, journals, and letters. And one character even records his diary entries using a device called a phonograph—modern technology for the 1890s.

Accounting for a Count

A count is a type of European noble, a person with great wealth and power who can pass his title on to his children. Some counts also ruled over large areas of land. But why did Dracula have the title of "count"?

As a count, Dracula would have the money to own a large castle, hire servants, buy a home in England, and easily travel across Europe. His money helped him hire lawyers like Jonathan Harker, the first character readers meet in the book *Dracula*. Since the count is obviously a wealthy man, Harker doesn't hesitate to visit him in Transylvania. By giving Dracula such an important title, Bram Stoker shows us why the characters in his novel trusted such a strange and scary person.

Harker describes his visit to Transylvania to meet Count Dracula. He notices that people are scared when he mentions Dracula and his castle. One woman even begs him not to go,

warning him about evil things that happen at the castle. But Harker does go there, and soon he learns that the count is a strange man.

Dracula is tall, thin, and pale, and dressed completely in black. When he shakes Harker's hand, the count's skin is icy cold, but his grip is so strong, the young lawyer winces in pain. Later, Harker notices the count's long, pointed fingernails, his hairy palms, and sharp teeth.

As the days pass, Harker learns even more odd things about Dracula. When the count stands in front of a mirror, he doesn't have a reflection. And when Harker accidentally cuts himself while shaving, the count grabs for his throat hungrily. Dracula pulls back only when he touches the small cross Harker wears around his neck. Later that same day, Harker realizes that all the castle doors are locked. He is Dracula's prisoner.

One evening, Harker watches in horror as Dracula climbs out a window and crawls down the wall of the castle headfirst, like a lizard.

He now realizes the count is even stranger than he had ever imagined. Harker begins to explore the castle, looking for a way to escape.

Several weeks pass, and Dracula makes clear he is not going to let Harker leave. One day, while exploring the castle again, Harker finds a room that contains fifty coffins filled with earth. Inside one of them, lying on a pile of dirt, is the count. His eyes are open, but he does not move.

Almost a week later, Harker returns to the room and again sees Dracula. This time, there is fresh blood on his face, and his whole body seems to be filled with blood.

Dracula is shipping all fifty coffins to England. When workmen come to remove them, Harker tries to rush outside, but he doesn't manage to escape. The men carry out the coffins, but Harker is left behind, trapped in the castle.

The next part of the story takes place in London, England. The readers meet Mina Murray, who will later marry Jonathan Harker. They also meet Mina's friend Lucy Westenra and the three men who would like to marry her: Arthur Holmwood, Dr. John Seward, and an American named Quincey Morris. Much of the story is told through Dr. Seward's diary entries.

In some of them, Seward describes an odd patient named Renfield in the hospital where he works. The man eats spiders, insects, and birds because he thinks they give him a special energy. As *Dracula* unfolds, it turns out that Renfield is under a spell cast by Dracula. Renfield calls him his master and can sense when he is near.

As the summer passes, Mina goes to visit Lucy in Whitby. Mina is worried because Jonathan has not returned from Transylvania. Meanwhile, the newspaper reports that a mysterious ship had arrived in port with no sailors on board.

The only person left was the captain. He was dead and tied to the ship's steering wheel. The ship had been carrying wooden boxes filled with earth.

On a night soon after the ship reached Whitby, Mina discovers that Lucy has left her bed. Mina searches for her friend and finds her outside the church. The next day, Mina notices two small bite marks on Lucy's neck.

By then, Mina had learned that Jonathan had somehow gotten out of Transylvania, though he was quite sick. Mina travels to Hungary to bring him back to England. She can see that he has experienced something awful, but he refuses to talk about it.

Back in Whitby, Lucy has been ill ever since the night Mina found her by the church. Arthur Holmwood is now engaged to Lucy, and he writes Dr. Seward to ask him to come see her. Seward can't find a reason why Lucy is so pale and lacking energy. He asks a former teacher of his, Dr. Abraham Van Helsing, to come examine Lucy.

As Van Helsing sees Lucy grow sicker, he realizes that she has been bitten by a vampire. Several weeks pass, and Seward and Van Helsing notice her teeth growing longer and sharper.

Before she can bite anyone, Lucy dies. But Van Helsing knows that since she is a vampire, she will come back to life seeking blood. Van Helsing, Seward, Holmwood, and Quincey Morris go to the graveyard where she is buried. The men drive a stake through Lucy's heart, cut off her head, and fill her mouth with garlic.

By then, Mina and Jonathan Harker have returned to England and are married. When they had first arrived, Jonathan was sure he had seen Count Dracula walking the streets. But he looked much younger than he had in Transylvania. Mina shares Harker's diary with Van Helsing, and the doctor realizes that Count Dracula must be the vampire who bit Lucy.

Together, Van Helsing, the Harkers, Seward, Holmwood, and Morris begin to hunt for Dracula. They rush to find all the coffins Dracula has hidden in homes around the city of London. Each of them is a secret hiding place for the count. The vampire hunters find many of the coffins and place religious items in them, to keep Dracula from using the coffins.

The search for Dracula becomes even more important after Dracula bites Mina and forms a special bond with her. She can sense what the count is doing and where he goes. The vampire hunters realize they must find and kill Dracula before Mina dies. Otherwise, she will become a vampire, too.

After Van Helsing hypnotizes her, Mina reveals that Dracula has boarded a ship and is leaving England. She joins the men as they set off to find him. Reaching Transylvania, the men find the wagon carrying Dracula back to his castle. They open the lid to his coffin.

In an instant, Jonathan Harker slits Dracula's throat, while Morris stabs the vampire through the heart. The count turns to dust before their eyes, and then the dust disappears. Dracula is dead.

CHAPTER 5
Dracula Appears!

Bram Stoker was not sure how people would react to *Dracula*. He told a friend he didn't think people would remember it after it was published. But some critics really liked the book.

Gothic Novels

Tales filled with spooky castles and ruined churches started becoming popular in Europe during the eighteenth century. Those buildings were sometimes made in an architectural style known as Gothic, and the books that featured them became known as Gothic novels.

These spooky stories often had mysterious villains, ghosts, or witches. In many of them, a hero saved a young woman from danger by the end of the book.

Many people believe Dracula is a Gothic novel because it features Dracula's castle, the creepy homes where his coffins are hidden, and the ruins of the Whitby church. And the story certainly shows an evil villain out to harm innocent young women.

But in other ways, Dracula is not a typical Gothic novel. Mina is not helpless. She helps save herself from the vampire. Several of the vampire hunters are scientists who use the latest technology of their day, including telegrams, typewriters, and the phonograph. Bram Stoker's book was a new kind of Gothic novel.

One newspaper compared the count's story to *Frankenstein* and the tales of horror and suspense that had been written by the American writer Edgar Allan Poe. Another critic wrote that some parts of the book so disgusted him, he read them quickly. But overall, the book gripped his attention and he applauded the novel. He warned parents, though, to keep the scary story away from children!

In 1899, *Dracula* first appeared in the United States. Bram's novel was published one chapter at a time, just like the penny dreadfuls, and printed in several newspapers. The entire book was published in 1899. In 1900, one newspaper called it one of the most famous

books of the year. Bram may not have thought his vampire tale was memorable, but US readers loved it, too!

When *Dracula* was first published, the book did not have any pictures. People didn't get their first look at the count until 1901. A version of the book published that year in England had a drawing of the vampire climbing down a wall of his castle. Dracula crawls down headfirst, like a lizard. He wears a long cape that looks like bat wings. In the illustration, Dracula's hairline along his forehead forms a point known as a widow's peak.

DRACULA

6d.

"
BRAM
STOKER

6d.

WESTMINSTER
Archibald Constable & Co Ltd
2 WHITEHALL GARDENS

Edgar Allan Poe (1809–1849)

Edgar Allan Poe was born in Boston, Massachusetts, and grew up in Richmond, Virginia. He published his first collection of poems when he was just eighteen years old, and went on to become the first American author to earn a living by writing. He later became famous for frightening stories that influenced many other writers. In one of them, "The Tell-Tale Heart," the narrator murders a man, and then is convinced the victim's heart is nearby and still beating. The sound of the beating heart drives him to confess to the murder.

Poe also sometimes wrote about people who seem to be dead but come back to life. In "The Fall of the House of Usher," the narrator helps his friend Roderick Usher bury his dead twin sister. But after about a week passes, the sister leaves her tomb. She had been buried alive.

Edgar Allan Poe is considered the creator of the first detective story, "The Murders in the Rue Morgue." He was also a critic, an editor, and a poet who is probably most famous for the poem "The Raven."

The next time anyone caught a glimpse of the Dracula character was in 1922. A German film company released a vampire movie that year titled *Nosferatu*. Like other movies at the time, *Nosferatu* was filmed in black and white, and it did not have sound. Parts of the story were told by words printed on a black background, called title cards, which were shown in between the action on the screen.

The company did not have legal permission to film the story the way that Bram Stoker told it in his book *Dracula*. So it changed the names of the characters. Count Dracula became Count Orlok, and Mina was renamed Ellen. The story, though, closely matched many parts of Stoker's book, and most people knew that the movie was retelling the story of *Dracula*.

Stoker's wife, Florence, was not too happy with *Nosferatu*. Mrs. Stoker had legal control over her husband's works. (Bram Stoker had died in 1912.) She demanded that the German film company pay for using the story. German courts agreed with her, but the company didn't have enough money to pay. So, Mrs. Stoker ordered all copies of

Florence Balcombe Stoker

Nosferatu destroyed. And most were. But one did reach the United States. The film was shown there for the first time in 1929.

CHAPTER 6
Dracula Comes to Life

While Mrs. Stoker did not approve of the German film version of her husband's book, she did let Bram's novel be turned into a play.

That version of *Dracula* meant fans could get their thrills and chills seeing the count "live" onstage.

Bram Stoker After Dracula

Before Bram Stoker died in 1912, he wrote several more books filled with horror and the supernatural.

- *The Jewel of Seven Stars* (1903): This time, the scary creature is a mummy.

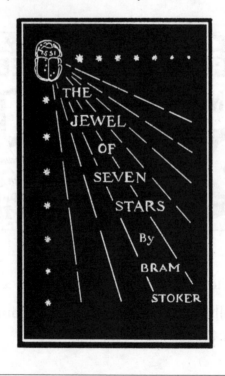

- *The Lady of the Shroud* (1909): A young woman named Teuta sleeps in a coffin and pretends to be a vampire. Teuta wants to scare away people who dislike her father.

- *The Lair of the White Worm* (1911): A tall, thin noblewoman is actually the human form of a giant flesh-eating snake.

- *Dracula's Guest and Other Weird Stories* (1914): In the title story, an unnamed Englishman travels to Transylvania and is caught in a storm. He seeks shelter by a large tomb. After a bolt of lightning destroys the tomb, he learns that the person he had traveled to Transylvania to meet is Count Dracula. This story was a part of the original Dracula book that Stoker did not use.

The play *Dracula* was first performed in 1924 in London. An actor named Hamilton Deane helped shape the image of Count Dracula that is so well known today. Stoker only once mentions Dracula wearing a cloak, which is like a cape.

Hamilton Deane

Onstage, Deane had the count wear a black cape with a high collar. The cape could sweep out on either side, making it look like bat wings. Deane also played Dracula as a gentleman wearing a tuxedo. And this count did not have hairy palms, pointed fingernails, or fangs. Onstage, Count Dracula looked like a true nobleman.

Deane had to trim much of the action from the original book so that the story would work as a play. His version takes place only in

London, and the character of Mina Harker is a combination of the book's Mina and her friend Lucy. But the changes didn't hurt the play's success. Audiences across England loved Deane's version of *Dracula*. It was so popular, he had three different groups of actors performing it in different theaters at the same time! At some shows, people screamed in horror or fainted as they watched the vampire approach his victims.

Hamilton Deane hired a nurse to come to the theater to take care of anyone who got sick.

In 1927, New York theater producer Horace Liveright saw *Dracula* in London. He decided to bring the play to the United States. To play Count Dracula, Liveright hired an actor named Bela Lugosi. He was not well known then in the United States. And he did not speak English well. But Lugosi was from Hungary, and his accent was perfect for the role. He eagerly agreed to take the part.

Dracula had its first US stage performance on October 5, 1927, in New York City. Liveright also had nurses in the theater to look after anyone who fainted. Some people suspected that not all the fainting was real. They thought that Liveright may have hired people to pretend to be scared— so scared that they fainted.

Bela Lugosi: The Man Who Played Dracula (1882–1956)

Many actors have played the role, but to Dracula fans, Bela Lugosi is the one true count. His real name was Béla Ferenc Dezső Blaskó, and he was born in Lugos, Hungary. (The town is now called Lugoj and is part of Romania—and it's not far from Transylvania!) He became an actor as a young man and changed his last name to Lugosi in honor of his hometown.

Lugosi traveled to New York in 1921 and soon began acting onstage there. He barely knew any English at the time, but he learned his lines by memorizing the sound of the words he spoke onstage. When he played Dracula in the 1931 movie, Lugosi added his own touch to the count's look. For two scenes, Lugosi wore a star-shaped medallion around his neck. Today, the medallion is still considered an important part of the costume for anyone who wants to dress as Dracula. Lugosi appeared in many movies after he made Dracula, but he is best known for playing the world's most famous vampire.

The American version of *Dracula* was a success. It played in New York for more than six months. The show also traveled to theaters across the country. Bela Lugosi sometimes played Dracula onstage, but other actors took on the role as well. Lugosi and some of the other actors also performed part of the play on the radio.

Carl Laemmle Jr.

Carl Laemmle Jr., who ran Universal Pictures at the time, saw *Dracula* while it was still playing in New York. His father had started Universal with other movie producers in 1912, but later the elder Laemmle bought the whole company. Universal had already had two big hits with scary movies: *The Hunchback of Notre Dame* and *The Phantom of the Opera*. Carl Laemmle Jr. thought *Dracula* could be another movie success.

In 1930, Universal Pictures bought the legal rights to make a film version of *Dracula*. Since the filming of the silent movie *Nosferatu*, studios had started making movies with sound. *Dracula* would be among the first horror "talking pictures."

CHAPTER 7
"I Never Drink . . . Wine"

Carl Laemmle Jr. thought the role of Count Dracula would be perfect for Lon Chaney, an American actor who had starred in some Universal films. But Lon Chaney was not available to play Dracula, so he chose Bela Lugosi for the role. He also hired several people to write a new version of *Dracula* for the screen. Lucy and Mina were once again two separate characters, rather than merged in a single character as they had been onstage. But Mina's character became the daughter of Dr. John Seward. Arthur Holmwood and Quincey Morris were not a part of the movie story, but the Van Helsing character was.

The movie was directed by Tod Browning,

Tod Browning

who had already shown talent for making creepy movies. In 1927, he directed *London After Midnight*, set partly in a bat-filled house where a murder had taken place. Years earlier, Browning had wanted to direct a film of *Dracula*. But Carl Laemmle Sr. was not a fan of horror stories and said no. Now the director could finally make his *Dracula*—and with sound!

In Bram Stoker's book, the count is clearly a frightening character. But early ads for the Universal Pictures film suggested that Dracula was almost

LON CHANEY
IN
London
After
Midnight

Metro-Goldwyn-Mayer

a romantic figure, whom women could not resist. Some people at Universal realized their audiences liked scary movies, and the ads for the film were changed to describe *Dracula* as "Weird! Terrifying! Sinister! Fascinating!"

As in the book, this version of *Dracula* opens in Transylvania. Renfield, not Jonathan Harker, is the lawyer who comes to Count Dracula's castle. He is there to discuss property the count wants to buy in London. The vampire smiles as a wolf howls in the distance. "Listen to them," he says to Renfield. "Children of the night. What music they make!" In another famous scene, Dracula is offered a drink. He replies, "I never drink . . . wine." This is Dracula's way of saying he does not need the food and drink humans enjoy. All he really needs is blood!

Universal's *Dracula* earned $120,000 in just eight days after it opened in 1931, a time when movie tickets cost about twenty-five cents each! The astonishing success of *Dracula* showed how much people enjoyed being scared while sitting in a dark movie theater. That summer, Universal Pictures began filming another well-known horror story: *Frankenstein* was released in November 1931. It was also a huge hit.

Ghost Artists

When Dracula admires the wolves he called "children of the night" howling outside his castle, he's not hearing a real animal. The howls came from what was then called a ghost artist. That's an actor who doesn't appear on-screen and provides the voice for one who is on-screen. For *Dracula*, D. G. Del Valle made the wolf noises, as well as the sounds of other animals: owls, bats, and frogs. Del Valle could also sound like different birds and donkeys or imitate a crying baby.

When the women in *Dracula* screamed, Universal turned to Sarah Schwartz. She has sometimes been called a scream queen, because she was so good at screaming! Her voice was used in many Universal films. Carl Laemmle Sr. said Schwartz would always have a job at Universal, providing the screams for other actors.

Sarah Schwartz

In 1938, theaters began showing double features of *Dracula* and *Frankenstein* together. In some cities, thousands of people lined up to see the frightening films.

CHAPTER 8
Counting on the Count

While Count Dracula dies at the end of the 1931 film, the interest in vampires certainly didn't. Bela Lugosi made another vampire movie in 1935 for a different studio. And in 1936, Universal released its second Dracula movie, *Dracula's Daughter*. The count does not appear in the film. Instead, it focuses on his daughter,

Countess Zaleska. *Dracula's Daughter* was so scary, one newspaper warned parents to not bring their children to see it.

During the 1940s, Universal made several more movies about Dracula, with different actors playing the famous vampire. One of those actors was Lon Chaney Jr. He had already played the Mummy, the Wolf Man, and Frankenstein's monster for Universal Pictures. In 1943, he starred in *Son of Dracula*. The movie was not as popular as the original, but the character of Dracula went on to appear as one of many monsters in the Universal films *House of Frankenstein* and *House of Dracula*. John Carradine played the count in both movies and in some later Dracula films as well.

In 1948, Bela Lugosi once again played the part that made him famous. Lugosi appeared as Count Dracula in *Bud Abbott and Lou Costello Meet Frankenstein*. Abbott and Costello were a popular comedy team at the time. The film also featured other monsters such as the Wolf Man and Frankenstein's monster.

Lon Chaney Jr. in
Son of Dracula

The movie was a combination of comedy and horror that scared audiences and also managed to make them laugh.

By the 1950s, US film companies were not making many vampire movies. But the British company Hammer Films thought people were still very interested in horror movies. Hammer made a deal with Universal Pictures to begin making movies about Dracula in England.

In 1958, English actor Christopher Lee played the vampire. But filmmaking had changed since the first Dracula movie had been made. Many films were now in color. In *Horror of Dracula*,

Christopher Lee in *Horror of Dracula*

moviegoers saw bright red blood dripping from Dracula's fangs for the first time.

In *Horror of Dracula*, much of the story focuses on Van Helsing and his hunt for the count. Dracula does not have all the spooky powers he has in Bram Stoker's book. He does not turn into a bat or disappear in a cloud of mist. But he is still hungry for blood, and he bites both Lucy and Mina. In the end, Dracula turns to dust when Van Helsing pulls back a curtain to let in sunlight.

Christopher Lee:
Another Popular Dracula (1922–2015)

Bela Lugosi was the most famous Dracula on-screen, but Christopher Lee might have been the scariest. The actor was six feet four, towering over both his victims and his hunters. And with his fangs dripping blood, no one could forget what Dracula craved most. Lee made his first movie in 1948 and appeared in many movies and TV shows before playing Dracula for the first time. Fans loved him in the role, and he went on to play the count a total of ten times. Years after Lee's last Dracula film, one fan bought a cape he wore as Dracula for about $41,000!

Christopher Lee is well known for playing Count Dooku in two Star Wars films. He also played the evil wizard Saruman in *The Lord of the Rings* and *The Hobbit* movies.

The movie opened first in England and was just called *Dracula*. A sign outside the theater used red lights to make it look like blood was dripping from Dracula's teeth. Another sign warned people: "DON'T DARE SEE IT ALONE!"

A few months later, Universal showed the film in the United States. It was now called *Horror of Dracula*. Through the early 1970s, Hammer Films made many more Dracula movies, with Christopher Lee usually playing the vampire.

In 1972, an African American cast starred in *Blacula*, the story of an African prince who is turned into a vampire by Dracula. William Marshall played the new vampire, named Blacula, who comes to Los Angeles and meets a woman who was his wife in a past life. Blacula turns her into a vampire, hoping they can live together forever. A second Blacula movie titled *Scream Blacula Scream* followed in 1973.

In 1979, Universal Pictures returned to Dracula. Two years before, New York producers had staged a new show of the play that had been such a hit during the 1920s. The new *Dracula* starred Frank Langella as the count.

Frank Langella as Dracula

The sets were in black and white and had images of bats and skulls painted on them. Universal then made a film based on the play, with Langella again playing Dracula. This count does not have fangs, but he does crawl down his castle wall, as in the book. It shows Dracula struggling with being undead. This *Dracula* is part horror story and part love story. And it reveals how people keep finding different ways to tell the tale of Bram Stoker's vampire.

CHAPTER 9
Dracula Lives!

The popularity of Dracula has let vampires of all sorts step out of the shadows and gain attention. Like Bram Stoker, other authors have found success creating their own vampires. In 1976, Anne Rice published the first of many books about a vampire named Lestat, a character who is part of a long line of vampires that dates back thousands of years to ancient Egypt.

Anne Rice

In 2005, Stephenie Meyer published *Twilight*, a vampire story about high school–aged teens who fall in love. Their story continued for three more books. And since 1979, even younger readers have enjoyed the stories of Bunnicula, who was created by Deborah and James Howe. This rabbit has fangs that it uses to suck the juice out of vegetables!

Stephenie Meyer

Like Dracula, other vampires have been the subject of popular movies, and some have appeared on TV, too. During the 1960s, the vampire Barnabas Collins was a main character in the daytime show *Dark Shadows*. The show ran for six years, and at its peak of success, twenty million viewers tuned in each day. A new version of *Dark Shadows* was briefly broadcast at night in 1991, and the original show was turned into a movie in 2012, starring Johnny Depp.

More recently, vampires have been featured in movies and television shows including *Buffy the Vampire Slayer, The Vampire Diaries,*

Dark Shadows' Barnabas Collins

and the *Twilight* movies. Several of Anne Rice's vampire stories have also been turned into films. The first, *Interview with the Vampire*, was released in 1994 and featured Tom Cruise and Brad Pitt.

Vampires in general, and Dracula in particular, have also appeared in comic books. Marvel  Comics featured Dracula in a series of comic books published during the 1970s, and then again in four issues of a series called *X-Men: Apocalypse vs Dracula*, published in 2006.

Images of Dracula can be found in many different places. In 1997, a photo of Bela Lugosi playing Dracula was printed on a US postage stamp. It was one of a series of five stamps honoring the famous Universal Pictures movie monsters.

Since 1972, millions of young children have enjoyed watching the *Sesame Street* character Count von Count. He wears a costume similar to Bela Lugosi's in the 1931 movie. He sounds a bit like the famous actor, too. Count von Count lives in a castle that is filled with bats. He loves to count and often counts his bats. The count has a girlfriend named Countess von Backwards who—naturally—counts backwards.

And cereal lovers have their own version of Dracula in Count Chocula, a chocolate-flavored cereal with a drawing on the box of a Dracula-like figure near his castle.

Vampire stories have been told all over the world, and it's easy to see why these creatures of the night are as popular as ever. But it was Bram Stoker who created the most famous vampire of all. His *Dracula*—like the character of the count himself—lives on.

A Castle Fit for a Count

A popular spot for Dracula fans visiting Transylvania today is the Hotel Castel Dracula. It was built during the 1980s on the Tihuta Pass, the real name for the spot Bram Stoker called Borgo Pass. The pass was near where Stoker placed the count's home.

The hotel is not an actual part of Dracula's story, but there is one place that just may be: Bran Castle sits on a hill in Bran, Romania. The castle was built during the fourteenth century. The people who run the castle today say that Stoker saw a drawing of it while he was writing *Dracula*. His description of the count's castle is said to be based on that drawing of Bran Castle.

Bibliography

*Books for young readers

Finn, Anne-Marie. "Whose Dracula Is it Anyway? Deane, Balderston and the 'World Famous Vampire Play.'" https://kutztownenglish. files.wordpress.com/2015/09/jds_v1_1999_finn.pdf.

Greshko, Michael. "Why Female Vampire Bats Donate Blood to Friends." *National Geographic*, November 17, 2015. https://news.nationalgeographic.com/2015/11/151117-vampire-bats-blood-food-science-animals/.

*Knox, Barbara. *Castle Dracula: Romania's Vampire Home.* New York: Bearport Publishing, 2005.

Leatherdale, Clive. *Dracula: The Novel and the Legend: A Study of Bram Stoker's Gothic Masterpiece.* Wellingborough, England: Aquarian Press, 1985.

Maberry, Jonathan. *Vampire Universe: The Dark World of Supernatural Beings That Haunt Us, Hunt Us, and Hunger for Us.* New York: Citadel Press, 2006.

*Mason, Jennifer. *Vampire Myths.* New York: Gareth Stevens Publishing, 2018.

McGarry, Marion. "Cholera, Sligo and the Shaping of Dracula: Stories of Victims Being Buried Alive Haunt Bram Stoker's Mother." *Independent.ie*, November 10, 2018, https://www. independent.ie/entertainment/books/cholera-sligo-and-the-shaping-of-dracula-stories-of-victims-being-buried-alive-haunted-bram-stokers-mother-37508980.html.

Miller, Elizabeth. *Dracula's Homepage*. "Bram Stoker, Vampires and Dracula." http://www.ucs.mun.ca/~emiller/bram_vampires_drac.html.

*Niver, Heather Moore. *Was Count Dracula Real?* New York: Enslow Publishing, 2017.

Polidori, John. *The Vampyre.* http://knarf.english.upenn.edu/Polidori/vampyre.html.

Scivally, Bruce. *Dracula FAQ: All That's Left to Know About the Count from Transylvania.* Milwaukee, WI: Backbeat Books, 2015.

Skal, David J. *Something in the Blood: The Untold Story of Bram Stoker, the Man Who Wrote Dracula.* New York: Liveright, 2016.

Stamp, Jimmy. "Why Does Dracula Wear a Tuxedo? The Origins of Bram Stoker's Timeless Vampire." *Smithsonian.com*, October 31, 2012, https://www.smithsonianmag.com/arts-culture/why-does-dracula-wear-a-tuxedo-the-origins-of-bram-stokers-timeless-vampire-101868474/.

Stoker, Bram. *Dracula.* Ware, England: Wordsworth Editions, 1993.

Wolf, Leonard. *Dracula: The Connoisseur's Guide.* New York: Broadway Books, 1997.

WATER DAMAGE
OCT 22